STUDIES IN E

This series, spec ..."
Society, provide.   .he
key themes of econo   ces
have recently been m   ant
debate.

Originally entitled 'Studies in Economic History', in 1974 the series had its scope extended to include topics in social history, and the new series title, 'Studies in Economic and Social History' signalises this development.

The series gives readers access to the best work done, helps them to draw their own conclusions in major fields of study, and by means of the critical bibliography in each book guides them in the selection of further reading. The aim is to provide a springboard to further work rather than a set of pre-packaged conclusions or short-cuts.

ECONOMIC HISTORY SOCIETY

The Economic History Society, which numbers over 3,000 members, publishes the *Economic History Review* four times a year (free to members) and holds an annual conference. Inquiries about membership should be addressed to the Assistant Secretary, Economic History Society, Peterhouse, Cambridge. Full-time students may join the Society at special rates.

STUDIES IN ECONOMIC AND SOCIAL HISTORY

Edited for the Economic History Society by L.A. Clarkson

PUBLISHED

OTHER TITLES ARE IN PREPARATION

Industry in Tudor and Stuart England

Prepared for
The Economic History Society by

D. C. COLEMAN

Professor of Economic History
in the University of Cambridge

**MACMILLAN
EDUCATION**

First published 1975
Reprinted 1983, 1987

Published by
MACMILLAN EDUCATION LTD
Houndmills, Basingstoke, Hampshire RG21 2XS
and London
Companies and representatives
throughout the world

Printed in Hong Kong

ISBN 0-333-14351-5

Contents

Note on References

References in the text within square brackets refer to the numbered items in the Select Bibliography, e.g. [33]. Other references in the text, numbered consecutively, relate to sources not in the Select Bibliography, detailed in the References section.

Editor's Preface

So long as the study of economic and social history was confined to a small group at a few universities, its literature was not prolific and its few specialists had no great problem in keeping abreast of the work of their colleagues. Even in the 1930s there were only two journals devoted exclusively to economic history and none at all to social history. But the high quality of the work of the economic historians during the inter-war period and the post-war growth in the study of the social sciences sparked off an immense expansion in the study of economic history after the Second World War. There was a great expansion of research and many new journals were launched, some specialising in branches of the subject like transport, business or agricultural history. Most significantly, economic history began to be studied as an aspect of history in its own right in schools. As a consequence, the examining boards began to offer papers in economic history at all levels, while textbooks specifically designed for the school market began to be published. As a specialised discipline, social history is an even more recent arrival in the academic curriculum. Like economic history, it, too, is rapidly generating a range of specialist publications. The importance of much of the recent work in this field and its close relationship with economic history have therefore prompted the Economic History Society to extend the scope of this series – formerly confined to economic history – to embrace themes in social history.

For those engaged in research and writing this period of rapid expansion of studies has been an exciting, if rather breathless one. For the larger numbers, however, labouring in the outfield of the schools and colleges of further education, the excitement of the explosion of research has been tempered by frustration arising from its vast quantity and, frequently, its controversial character. Nor, it must be admitted, has the ability or willingness of the academic historians to generalise and summarise marched in step with their enthusiasm for research.

The greatest problems of interpretation and generalisation have tended to gather round a handful of principal themes in economic and social history. It is, indeed, a tribute to the sound sense of economic and social historians that they have continued to dedicate their energies, however inconclusively, to the solution of these key problems. The results of this activity, however, much of it stored away in a wide range of academic journals, have tended to remain inaccessible to many of those currently interested in the subject. Recognising the need for guidance through the burgeoning and confusing literature that has grown around these basic topics, the Economic History Society hopes in this series of short books to offer some help to students and teachers. The books are intended to serve as guides to current interpretations in major fields of economic and social history in which important advances have recently been made, or in which there has recently been some significant debate. Each book aims to survey recent work, to indicate the full scope of the particular problem as it had been opened up by recent scholarship, and to draw such conclusions as seem warranted, given the present state of knowledge and understanding. The authors will often be at pains to point out where, in their view, because of a lack of information or inadequate research, they believe it is premature to attempt to draw firm conclusions. While authors will not hesitate to review recent and older work critically, the books are not intended to serve as vehicles for their own specialist views: the aim is to provide a balanced summary rather than an exposition of the author's own viewpoint. Each book will include a descriptive bibliography.

In this way the series aims to give all those interested in economic and social history at a serious level access to recent scholarship in some major fields. Above all, the aim is to help the reader to draw his own conclusions, and to guide him in the selection of further reading as a means to this end, rather than to present him with a set of pre-packaged conclusions.

M. W. FLINN
University of Edinburgh   *Editor*

1 Introduction: Industry in the Pre-Industrialised Economy

I

An initial question: how can one talk about 'industry' in a society often called 'pre-industrialised' or even 'pre-industrial'? Is this not an obvious absurdity? The concept of an industrialised society, brought into being by a process of industrialisation or, more dramatically, by what has come to be called an industrial revolution, must carry with it the corollary of a non-industrialised or pre-industrialised society. The definitions and the distinctions are not precise; they do not have universal applicability; they are chronologically blunt. As useful labels for differing economic and social patterns, however, they convey meanings which other sorts of labels – seventeenth century or twentieth century, Tudor England or Victorian England – fail to convey. Yet the two things co-existed: what for one purpose we label 'Tudor England', and what for another purpose we label 'pre-industrialised England'. The criteria and chronology are different, but it is important that we should remember their co-existence. The contours of the industrialised society are familiar in such features as urbanisation, mechanised manufacture, or the dominance of industry over agriculture. It is more important to recognise its fundamental economic characteristic: its dependence upon substantial investment in fixed capital, embodying technical devices which raise productivity to levels far higher than anything obtainable in the absence of that investment.

It is because this human achievement made its first massive appearance in manufacturing industry that we have come to think and speak of the sort of society built upon that achievement – whatever its political form or moral base – as industrialised. It does not mean that societies which preceded it had no industry, that they had no capital, or that they were devoid of capitalism. Nor does it mean that they were all the same. But it does imply that capital investment of this particular type was normally absent in the industrial activity of pre-industrialised economies. Naturally, there were exceptions. It is that pervasive absence, however, which constitutes the major distinguishing mark of industry before the Industrial Revolution, and which enables us to talk of industries in pre-industrialised societies.*

The dominance of agriculture in the pre-industrialised economy provides a second clue to the nature of industry in such a society. Much of it consisted of the direct processing of agricultural products in order to meet the three basic needs of life – food and drink, shelter, clothing. Milling and baking, brewing and distilling, from the products of the arable economy; the making of textiles, be it from wool or flax, or of leather from the skins and hides of the pastoral economy; the processing of wood from the forests, be it for house-building or shipbuilding or for charcoal: these were the fundamentals, far removed from the foundations of the modern industrialised economy – engineering, power, chemicals. Furthermore, these linkages between agriculture and industry were often so close that much manufacturing activity was carried on by people who also worked in agriculture. Productive processes were geared to the seasonality of the crops or were at the mercy of the weather, just as were harvests; much industrial labour was intermittent, seasonal, casual. Here and there, in particular regions or circumstances, something that began to look like a landless, industrial proletariat was beginning to emerge alongside the landless agricultural labourers; but for the most part this was not a characteristic feature of the pre-industrialised economy. Just as the lines between town and country, between rural and urban life, were often blurred, so were the lines between industrial and agrarian occupations. To talk of a distinct and separate 'industrial sector' would be anachronistic. Capital and labour alike were rarely as specific and particular as

* I prefer the term 'pre-industrialised' to 'pre-industrial' simply because the latter, despite its agreeably shorter form, does not convey the full meaning, does not allow that there can be industry without industrialisation.

today. A water-mill, for example, might be used for grinding grain to make flour or beating rags to make paper; a weaver would often work in the fields at harvest time, a clothier might also be a grocer or an innkeeper; a yeoman farmer might be a tanner of leather.

There remains one further feature, or, to be more accurate, a double-feature, to be emphasised as an essential ingredient of industry in the pre-industrialised society. Because technological advance was slow and therefore productivity-raising capital investment, embodying new technical methods, was rare, labour not only continued to be, but was normally seen to be, the most important factor in industrial production. Most industry was, in modern terminology, labour-intensive rather than capital-intensive. This had a number of important consequences, amongst them the fact that as international industrial competition intensified the workers' standard of living, already low, was put further at risk. But the very nature of this industrial development was in turn strongly influenced by the other aspect of this double feature: the existence in such societies of a reservoir of underemployed labour. The size varied from area to area, according to the nature of the agriculture practised or the structure of employment in particular regions; and, from time to time, according to the rise and fall of population. Its existence, however, was inherent in the nature of the agriculture of the day; in the very limitations of man's control over nature, which thus left economic life subject to many of its vagaries; and also in the prevalent social structure and attitudes, which saw the 'labouring poor' as the greater part of that politically voiceless multitude who provided the unskilled labour force and for whose ailing, idle or unemployed members the poor law was evolved. To the extent that this labour reserve continued or expanded, so long was the incentive to labour-replacing invention and innovation weakened, though certainly not removed; in so far as it contracted or lost its docile willingness to work, so was the incentive to productivity-increasing capital investment strengthened.

Nothing was ever so simple in reality. This is merely a rough model, designed to indicate some of the salient features of the pre-industrialised economy. It is built upon the assumption that

13

productive inputs, be they of labour or capital, were usually shifted according to costs, known or estimated, and profits, accruing or expected. There is enough contemporary evidence to suggest that such an assumption is not unrealistic. It is far from implying that men and women were constantly engaged in trying to maximise profits. The operations of the profit motive in industry were influenced, perhaps even more than today, by a complex of social, political and religious forces : by autocratic kingship; by the pre-emptive power of a status-oriented society; by acts of industrial policy often owing more to a concern with public order or social stability than to any understanding of the mechanics of economic growth; and, not least, by a civil war. Much is of necessity ignored in this brief coverage. The omissions include such matters as industrial policy, the wages of industrial workers, or the details of industrial finance. What it attempts to do is to provide a simple analysis of industrial organisation and change in Tudor and Stuart England considered as an example of the pre-industrialised economy.

II

Measured against the best practices of continental Europe, English industry at the end of the fifteenth century was backward. With the one major exception of woollen cloth, England's exports were those of a primary producer : raw wool, lead, tin, skins and hides. Although her great manufacture of woollen cloth had brought the country into the first league of industrial producers and traders, it is well to remember that, despite the high quality and renown of English broadcloth, much of the output was inferior in quality to the best products of the Italian and Flemish industries; that the boom in English cloth exports between 1450 and 1550 rested heavily on the cheaper sorts; and that in cloth dyeing and finishing techniques England was far behind the best continental practice. In mining and metallurgy the Germans were the masters, and in the course of the sixteenth century English governments tried hard – and with some success – to lure German skill and capital to this country. Over a range of other industries – paper, linen, silk, leather-working, hosiery, iron-founding, glass-making – English inferiority to French, Spanish, Italian,

14

Flemish, or German industries was manifest, not only in the quality of products, but in the country's dependence on imports either for the better quality of such wares or even for all of them. Nor was it merely a question of supply. English demand for many manufactured wares was very limited, for the simple reason that levels of wealth and income, as of culture and sophistication, of urban brilliance or mercantile glory were all inferior to those of the great centres of continental Europe.

If this was England's relative industrial situation when the Tudors came to the throne in 1485, it was in certain ways very different when the Stuarts left it in 1714. By then there were few industrial techniques which England had not secured from the outside world and in some cases substantially improved. The range of textiles had been extended, their output multiplied and their quality improved; a widespread stocking-knitting industry was feeding an export trade; the paper, linen and silk industries were all well-established, although still inferior in quality or output to French, Dutch or German counterparts. In mining and metallurgy the iron industry, though still inferior to that of Sweden – the greatest European iron producer of the day – had expanded enormously; the manufacture of metalwares had grown up in the West Midlands; and England had become almost certainly the biggest coal-producing and consuming country in Europe. A number of new industries had started, such as the manufacture of alum used in dyeing and tanning, and others which were direct or indirect results of the massive expansion of English overseas trade, for example, the processing of American tobacco, the refining of Caribbean sugar, or the printing of Indian calicoes; and, a very direct consequence, an enlarged ship-building industry. Succeeding waves of immigrants – German, Flemish, French, many of them Protestant refugees from religious persecution – had helped to transmit various continental techniques to England. Despite some continuing inferiorities in quality of output, English industry was in a stronger position relative to the outside world than it had been two centuries earlier : it had caught up technically, it had a wider base from which to advance, and, most important, it had a bigger and wealthier home market. Spanish, Italian and Flemish industries had declined; others had grown in France, Holland and Germany; and these were formidable competition for English manufacturers. But by the end of Stuart times, English industry was far better placed to meet such challenges than it had been at the beginning of Tudor times.

How had all this come about?

Before attempting to answer this question, two points must be stressed. First, the pleasing picture sketched above of industrial change, achievement and advance needs some drastic qualifications. In 1700, as in 1500, the making of woollen textiles, of one sort or another, was still the country's biggest manufacturing industry and their export still accounted for about 70 per cent, in value, of the country's total exports of its own produce, that is excluding re-exports. Moreover, no major technical innovation had significantly altered any of the chief processes of woollen textile production, nor had water power made any new contribution to those processes. Indeed, although the water-mill had come into use in various new manufacturing processes, for example, in the blast-furnace, the slitting-mill, and the paper-mill, human muscles were still the great prime mover of industry. Only at the very end of our period did a totally new sort of power, that of the atmospheric engine, make its appearance as a pumping device in mining. Only in the very last decade of the Stuart reigns was the power of an English river applied to a primary process in textile manufacture, namely silk-throwing [33]; and only then was success finally attained in efforts to smelt iron with coal instead of charcoal. These final achievements were indeed to have far-reaching consequences, but they lie outside our area of concern. The innovations will demand our attention, not least because such matters – and there were a few others – stand out in an age of technological conservatism. Industrial techniques were neither primitive nor stagnant, but they changed infrequently and patchily. In brief, for all the changes that had happened, the English economy was still of a pre-industrialised sort at the end of the period as at the beginning, and the expansion of its overseas trade had been far more striking than its industrial development. Perhaps there had been a 'commercial revolution'; there had certainly not been anything worth calling an 'industrial revolution'. When, therefore,

16

we come to consider the course of industrial change and to seek its causation, we must expect to find it less in major technical innovations than in other influences, be they of demand or supply, bearing upon the size and organisation of productive activity.

The second point to be stressed is one which applies to almost all attempts to examine the economic history of any country before very recent times: we have very few figures to go on. Because of this paucity of statistical data we can rarely measure output or employment, costs or profits, progress or decay. Nor can we normally hope to make the type of attribution of causality which modern techniques of econometrics permit for later periods of history, favoured with an abundance of statistics which it is not too great an offence to truth to call reliable. Fragmentary statistics survive for particular periods, for some products, for a town here or a port there, for specific enterprises; often they relate to overseas trade rather than to output or home sales; they are fraught with the problems of comparability peculiar to an era of numerous and diverse weights and measures. So our knowledge and analysis of England's early industrial history has to be conducted substantially by mixing literary evidence with some very partial quantitative evidence, in what one hopes to be judicious and scholarly proportions. Consequently the difficulty of distinguishing the typical from the exceptional, the average from the abnormal, is more than usually acute. Lack of regard for this problem has resulted in some very misleading statements about the course of English industrial development at this time.

III

The way in which any industrial activity is organised is substantially determined by the production techniques currently known to those engaged in it and by the size of the market served by it. In Tudor and Stuart England, three very broad forms of industrial organisations can be seen:
  (a) crafts (discussed in Chapter 2),
  (b) the domestic or 'putting-out' system (discussed in Chapter 3),
  (c) centralised production (discussed in Chapter 4).

This is certainly not a clear-cut set of categories; one pattern shades into another. But it has a rough correspondence with reality – which is as much as one can hope for – and can be used to demonstrate how, in the simplest of economic terms, elements affecting supply interacted with those of demand, to shape the structure and organisation of industry.

2 Crafts and Gilds

I

In this first category were all those craftsmen, artisans, workers of one sort or another, who made up what is sometimes called the 'handicraft' sector of the community. The essential unit of production was the individual skilled worker; according to the size of his business he was assisted by one or more unskilled or semi-skilled 'journeymen' as well as an apprentice or apprentices learning their craft. This was 'manufacture' in the most literal sense: simple hand tools, no capital plant, and no division of labour by process involving a central organising figure, as in the domestic or putting-out system. Some worked directly on the basic raw materials of this pre-industrialised society: the carpenters, coopers, wheelwrights and joiners who processed wood; the craftsmen of the leather industry – curriers, tawers, cordwainers, glovers or saddlers – an important group whose products finished up in a remarkable range of uses, from boots to buckets, from skirts to saddles; the masons and thatchers of the building trades; the bakers, butchers, brewers and others in victualling; and the men who worked with metals – farriers, plumbers, or pewterers, from the village blacksmith to the city goldsmith. It included, though decreasingly, some skilled workers in textiles, such as dyers or shearmen as well as the tailors who worked with the manufactured fabrics; and it comprehended a variety of service trades from barbers to stationers.

Such crafts were to be found throughout the economy; they were at the very core of life in towns; and they survived throughout the period. They were of great economic importance and, indeed, were to be so well into the nineteenth century, before the flood of factory-produced objects thinned the ranks of such workers. We cannot unfortunately measure their output; if this were possible we might well find that such work constituted the largest single source of industrial production. The greater part of the output was consumed at home though some entered into exports. As the volume of internal trade increased, more products of such craft activity were dispersed about the country, were sold at markets and fairs, and thus satisfied more than purely local needs.

II

Craft occupations of this sort have commonly been associated with the gilds. Many such gilds, medieval in origin, did indeed exist in towns all over the country, from the Cappers of Coventry to the Carpenters' Company of London, from the Company of Weavers, Fullers and Shearmen of Exeter to the Shoemakers of Chester. But it is important to understand that gilds were not in themselves units of functional economic organisation so much as methods of association and control or social foci of civic ceremony and ritual. They were not in themselves sources of finance, of credit or capital, though the kinship or friendship of members could facilitate the granting of trade credit. As a rough analogy with modern times, they carried out some of those economic functions today exercised by trade unions or employers' associations, not those performed by factories or by joint-stock companies. The origins of gilds need not concern us here. It is sufficient to emphasise that their most important economic function was their potential ability to control entry into a trade or craft and thus, by regulating the supply of labour, to maintain wages as well as standards of work. The normal method of regulation was to insist upon apprenticeship as a path to full membership of the gild; and this in turn might sometimes be the only formal path to the 'freedom' of the town and thus the right to carry on business there.

Clearly such arrangements for regulation could be expected to work at their best only so long as economic conditions remained fairly static. If either the labour supply or the demand for particular goods were to increase substantially, pressure for entry would mount or production would expand outside the gilds. This seems to have been happening by the beginning of the sixteenth century, and it led in England to a gradual and piecemeal decline in the power and authority of the gilds over the period as a whole – an historical experience significantly different from that which occurred in many parts of continental Europe. The decay of English gilds was probably hastened by the earlier move of the textile industry into rural areas, and by the failure of the urban-based gilds to establish their authority in such areas, although in some rural industries forms of gild control did continue to operate, for example that exercised in the cutlery industry in and around Sheffield by the Company of Hallamshire Cutlers. In London craft gilds came under the domination of mercantile gilds whose richer and more powerful members controlled either the markets or the raw materials of the craftsmen [10]. Thus, for example, at various dates between 1479 and 1517 the London leather craftsmen came under the aegis of the Leathersellers Company. More and more it was the richer mercantile elements of the so-called 'Livery' Companies which came to control the 'Commonalty', the craft element. The Grocers, the Merchant Taylors, the Haberdashers, the Goldsmiths, the Carpenters, and the rest of the London Companies, the majority of them incorporated by royal charter in the late fifteenth century (itself an expensive process dependent upon a wealthy group in the gild), survived to typify the gild structure in London. And they, in turn, and especially during the seventeenth century, gradually lost their economic *raison d'être* as real power came to rest with the great trading companies or with individual merchants. They prolonged their existence in an increasingly ornamental form, with their halls and feasts, but with diminished economic content.

Parallel with this process – and more to be found outside London – were different but similarly disrupting developments [9]. One gild encroached on another as crafts overlapped: brewers baked, tanners made shoes, glovers traded in leather. Carefully built up craft demarcations were broken down. Sometimes, under the impact of economic change, of intruding merchants and competition from outside, gilds set about amalgamating. Bakers linked with brewers, joiners with carpenters. But change was inevitably

21

patchy. In some provincial towns gilds remained alive and vigorous for much of the sixteenth century [12]. The state itself, however, intentionally or unintentionally, weakened gild power. Later Tudor attempts to limit the spread of rural industry in the interests of corporate towns gave the crucial powers of jurisdiction not to the gilds but to the Justices of the Peace; and their disposition to support, say, formal apprenticeship was never so strong as their concern with the maintenance of employment in the interest of social order. The English state, unlike some continental counterparts, did not rejuvenate gilds or endow them with powers of industrial regulation. On the contrary, Tudors and early Stuarts alike looked with successfully covetous eyes at their possibilities as a source of revenue. After Protector Somerset had taken his bite at the religious possessions of the gilds, Elizabeth and especially James I further weakened the effective power of the London gilds by selling grants of incorporation to all sorts of lesser handicrafts at an appropriate price. Thus were gilds tarred with the smelly brush of monopolies and patents, as sundry trivial trades were sold charters or split from dominating mercantile element. In many towns all that was left by the eighteenth century was a series of forms without content. Some gilds still functioned, enjoyed periods of prosperity, exercised their rights over limited areas. Many had vanished, others existed to feast, to argue about trivia, to try to control trades which had passed out of their grasp. Meanwhile, other manufacturing activities, such as iron-smelting or paper-making, had grown up virtually untouched by gilds. To take a final example, when we find in seventeenth-century Maidstone that all the trades of this flourishing Kentish market town are grouped into four gilds – Mercers, Drapers, Cordwainers, Victuallers – we may suspect decay. But when further investigation reveals that the Mercers included not only mercers and grocers, but also weavers, dyers, threadmakers, goldsmiths, physicians, surgeons and 'all petty chapmen', then we can be reasonably certain that economically meaningful gild life there was dead.

3   The Domestic or Putting-Out System

I

If the market for manufactured goods becomes sufficiently large and if the techniques of production are such that manufacture can be carried on in the homes of workers, then it is very probable that some sort of 'putting-out' or domestic system will emerge as a dominant form of industrial organisation in activities to which these demand and supply conditions apply. This generalisation is simply a particular variation on the famous theme, first enunciated by Adam Smith in the *Wealth of Nations*, that the division of labour is limited by the extent of the market. It can be made as an historical generalisition because the 'putting-out' phenomenon, in one guise or another, has been observed in certain industries in many countries and over several centuries. It has been seen in textiles, hosiery, lace, gloves, cutlery, nails, shoes, clothing, furniture, to name but some manufactures; it has been seen in thirteenth-century Flanders and in twentieth-century China; Europe, Asia, Africa and America have known, or still know, such arrangements in some industries. So its appearance in England is not a phenomenon which can be explained simply by reference to English conditions. Yet its particularly rapid development in England during our period is something which demands, in part at least, an English explanation.

First, however, it is useful to consider briefly the general conditions likely to favour the emergence of these arrangements. The techniques of production must be similar to those of handicraft industries in the sense that they can be carried on with simple tools capable of being stored and used in the workers' homes. Moreover, those tools must either be cheap enough to be within the purchasing power of the domestic worker, such as the simple hand-loom; or, like the knitting frame of the early hosiery

23

industry, such that they may be lent out without severe risk to the owner of loss or damage. The basic skills required must either be those customarily pursued in peasant households, such as spinning, or those readily learnable through some type of simple training or informal apprenticeship, as, for example, the methods of making the hand-forged nail. The processes of manufacture should not require close supervision, thus implying that the products should be of a fairly standardised nature. The raw materials or semi-finished goods entrusted to the domestic workers cannot be of great value, otherwise the risk of loss would be too high : the goldsmith's trade would hardly be a candidate for the putting-out system.

These conditions may be necessary, but they are not sufficient causes for the emergence of a putting-out system in an industry. There must be an effective demand for the goods in question greater than that which could be satisfied by artisan or handicraft production on a local basis. In order to discover whether potential demand could be made effective the requisite enterprise must be there to forge the vital link between commercial expansion and the re-organisation of production, and thus to feed the new markets. So it is usually merchant-entrepreneurs who are to be found exploiting the labour of a rural work-force by putting out wool for spinning or yarn for weaving, or iron for making up into small metal wares. Their role was essentially to organise and finance. The capital of such industries, because of the techniques involved, mainly took the form of raw materials, semi-finished goods, and stocks – what is sometimes called 'circulating' capital. So the main prop of the financial structure was the provision of working credit to cover the completion of the various processes up to the sale of the final product. As production increased and the organisation became more complex, more intermediaries were involved in this credit provision : wool-dealers, clothiers, cloth-factors, drapers, merchants. In this way an elaborate network of credit and debt linked up the various parts of industry, thus opening wider the channels of enterprise for the strong as well as setting traps for the weak. And this brings us to one of the most crucial conditions for these arrangements and also back to one of the basic circumstances of the pre-industrialised economy :

the existence of underemployed workers capable of taking on such work, poor, unorganised, eager to supplement their meagre earnings from agriculture. From this it follows that an increase in population in an area already engaged in manufacturing is likely to be peculiarly favourable to an extension of the system. Conversely, a decrease of population there would be peculiarly unfavourable and could, *if demand continued to grow*, stimulate the development of the one thing which must ultimately destroy the whole putting-out arrangements, namely the introduction of productivity-raising fixed capital such as power-driven machinery. So long as demand keeps up, so long as technology is unable to solve its problems and so long as the labour supply is adequate, in a new area if not in an old, so long will the putting-out arrangements survive. In our period it flourished; and nowhere more so than in the textile industry.

II

The substantial expansion of the textile industry in Tudor and Stuart times was effectively a continuation of trends already evident in fourteenth-century England. Hampered, indeed at times reversed during the first half of the fifteenth century, expansion set in again in the second half of the century. Thereafter it was sustained during the Tudor and early Stuart reigns by the big upsurge of population, providing just those circumstances of easy labour supply which, as we have seen, were especially conducive to the growth of the putting-out system. The enlarging demand came certainly from a massive growth in English overseas trade and very probably from an increase in the home market.

Exports of woollen cloth roughly trebled between the 1450s and 1550s. After this time, it is difficult to show the expansion in overseas textile sales in terms of numbers of cloths, because of the marked diversification in the types of fabrics made and exported. But two different indications can be used to show that growth continued. The total annual value of English textile exports (almost entirely pure woollens) was probably about £600,000 in the 1560s and 1570s; London's textile exports alone (of more diverse sorts of woollens and worsteds) were worth approximately £1½m. in the 1660s; and in the period from 1699 to 1701 total English textile exports (by now still mainly woollens and worsteds, but also a little linen and silk as well as hosiery) had an annual average value of about £3m. The other indicator is provided by the receipts of certain dues payable on cloths sold at the biggest cloth market in the country, Blackwell Hall in London [17]. These dues show a three-fold increase between the 1570s and the first decade of the eighteenth century. This is certainly an understatement of the true increase because it excludes certain types of textiles as well as those sold elsewhere. In *very* rough terms, the money value of English textile exports may have multiplied about fifteen-fold between 1485 and 1714; this is little more than a guess and is subject to wide margins of error. We do not know its relation to total output because we do not know the proportion of exports to sales on the home market, nor do we know how much of home demand was met by subsistence production which did not enter into the market at all. It seems likely that the latter shrank over the period and was of small consequence at the end; and unless we make the most unlikely assumption that the ratio of home consumption to total output fell from a high figure at the beginning of the period to a low figure at the end, then there must have been a similarly large increase in total production at least commensurate with that in exports. Such an increase over the period would therefore have exceeded the growth in population and the rise in industrial prices, both of which perhaps trebled. In brief, the industry seems to have achieved a greater and more diverse output per head of the population. How? What did it produce? And where?

The extension of the putting-out system in textiles was probably the main though not the sole route to this achievement. Textile production, it should be emphasised, was peculiarly compatible with this system – for two reasons. First, the whole sequence of manufacture could be split up into separate processes, thus achieving that greater degree of division of labour which facilitated the lowering of costs and raising of productivity. Second, although the cloth normally left the domestic sequence for some processes, such as fulling, dyeing or finishing, the basic processes of manufacture fitted in remarkably well with the family structure: children carded the wool; women spun it into yarn; men wove the fabric and did the finishing processes. Consequently the fixed costs of some central establishment were not normally worth incurring. They could in effect be passed on to the workers in their cottages. It is for this reason that the true significance of such celebrated early sixteenth-century textile entrepreneurs as John Winchcombe (Jack of Newbury) and William Stumpe – both renowned for having put many looms under one roof – lies in their uniqueness, in the very absence of imitators. They were, not to put too fine a point on it, boom-time freaks.

The system spread in three main areas of woollen textile production: the West Country, East Anglia, and, to a lesser extent, the West Riding of Yorkshire; in the linen and fustian* industry of Lancashire; and at the end of our period it appeared in the hosiery industry already developing in the East Midlands. The products of the woollen industry varied from region to region. Particular types of cloth had long been associated with particular areas, though sometimes the making of sorts which still bore names derived from one area were introduced into other areas. So there were not only Suffolk kerseys, (a light, cheap cloth bearing the name of a village in that county) but also Devonshire kerseys and Yorkshire kerseys – and they were by no means all the same. At the beginning of the period cloth-making was more widespread than it later became, and the putting-out organisations was not ubiquitous. Plenty of independent weavers were at work, in the West Riding of Yorkshire making their 'penistones' and 'northern dozens' [21], or amongst the weavers of Lancashire in the sixteenth century [22], weaving coarse linens or the types of cheap woollens known (to the confusion of historians) as 'cottons'. The putting-out arrangements were more fully developed in the West Country industry [23, 24], stretching from Gloucestershire, through Wiltshire and parts of Somerset, and down into Devonshire. Gloucestershire and Wiltshire, famous for broadcloths, already had the full range of the characteristic structure of this industry: at one end was the small quasi-independent weaver, struggling, often in debt to the wool or yarn merchants who supplied his raw material; at the other end was the rich

* A fabric with a linen warp and a cotton weft.

27

clothier, operating on a large scale, putting out wool to be carded and spun in the local villages, supplying yarn to the weavers, and seeing the cloth fulled and sheared, prior to sending it for sale in London. Such men, levering themselves up in the social scale by the money made in this business, married into the landowning gentry, as did their counterparts in the similarly organised industry of Suffolk [28] and northern Essex. An old-established area of broadcloth and kersey-making, this is a region in which enduring testimonies to cloth-making wealth still survive today, in the shape of numerous churches, like those at Lavenham, Long Melford or Dedham, re-built in the fifteenth and early sixteenth centuries.

Just why the industry came to be concentrated in these particular areas is not easy to determine. Certainly by this period it was not because of locally available wool supplies. Such wool-producing counties as Lincolnshire had little or no cloth-making; conversely, such major manufacturing areas as Devon or Suffolk imported their wool from sundry parts of the country [16]. Yet continuity or inertia – call it what you will – plays some part in influencing location; and the availability of raw-material supplies at one period in history has sometimes resulted in the continuance of industry in a particular area long after that influence on its location has changed or disappeared. Without its sixteenth-century linen industry, for example, Lancashire might never have developed its later and more famous cotton industry [25]; the availability of the long, coarse wools of many an upland region were the original bases of the cloth made in Welsh border areas [27] and the south-west. But in an expanding, labour-intensive, putting-out industry, the location of commercial production was more and more dependent not on raw-material supply but on labour supply. This in turn was connected with the amount of employment or underemployment generated by the type of agriculture practised in a particular region, and with the sorts of land inheritance systems which facilitated or impeded the sub-division of peasant holdings and hence the ease or otherwise with which a settlement, however small, might be obtained in the area. Dr Joan Thirsk has argued [1] that the so-called 'wood-pasture' regions of the country, where arable farming was subordinate to dairying, where much land was enclosed and holdings small and readily

28

obtainable, were peculiarly favourable to such industrial development. Population multiplied, by natural increase and by immigration, the underemployed labour force grew, and the earnings of industrial work became vital supports of the community. The hypothesis goes a long way towards explaining the concentration in some of the textile areas – those of Yorkshire, Somerset, the Kentish Weald, or the Stour valley area of Suffolk, with its remarkably high population density in the early sixteenth century – but it is probably only a partial answer to a problem which needs further investigation.

By the end of the period many of the older, scattered cloth-making towns and areas had decayed. As new centres like Leeds and Halifax rose so did the older, gild-dominated towns such as Beverley and York, lose their former pre-eminence. Cloth-making contracted in Surrey, Hampshire and Kent [45], where Wealden clothiers and workers complained bitterly of poverty and decay. In the three big areas the putting-out system was further expanded and consolidated, gradually ousting the independent weavers and making headway even in the West Riding. But alongside this tightening grip of the system, there was a marked change in the nature of the output, a diversification of the types of textiles produced. This took a number of forms, but one common thread of causation runs through them all: foreign influences. Sometimes it arose from deliberate attempts, initiated by merchants trying to meet overseas demands, to copy competing fabrics; sometimes it was the import of foreign fabrics which sold well on the home market that stimulated domestic efforts to imitate these fashionable things – often aided by a government which saw that, by erecting tariffs, it might combine industrial protection with much-needed revenue. These demands could not so readily have been met, however, with the dissemination of skills which came from the successive waves of immigrants to England. Just as the establishment of the American colonies owed much to refugees from English religious intolerance, so English economic life was in debt to continental Europe's religious intolerance which drove a variety of skilled craftsmen and traders across the Channel.

Chronologically, the first influence in this period came with the introduction of what contemporaries called the 'new draperies'

[16, 18, 19, 28, 29]. The older sorts of cloth – which in turn inevitably came to be known as 'old draperies' – were chiefly pure woollens, that is in warp and weft, made of short-stapled wool which had been carded. The 'new draperies' were worsteds – made of long-stapled wool which had been combed – or, more commonly, mixtures of woollen and worsted yarns or even of worsted and silk. Moreover, they were generally lighter, more colourful, more varied, often cheaper and sometimes less durable. They thus brought in a higher replacement demand. Technically, they were derived from continental European textile-manufacturing practices. So, not surprisingly, their introduction into England was largely a product of the migration in the 1560s and 1570s of Protestants fleeing from Spanish Catholic persecution in the Netherlands.

'Much wool is turned into bayes, sayes, grograines, rash, and other kinds of foreign wares of late years made here by divers workmen straingers that are come over and do inhabit here.'[1] Thus did the governor of the Russia Company report to its chief agent in Russia in 1591 of the effects of this immigration. The refugees settled mainly in eastern and southern England, in Norwich, Colchester, Canterbury and some other towns. By the very nature of early textile manufacture, the learning of different ways of carrying out such time-honoured hand processes as weaving demands a special impulse. So the natives had to be taught by the immigrants and gradually the new ways caught on. By the end of the seventeenth century the new draperies were no longer new. Under sundry curious names they had been naturalised: bays and says in Essex, with Colchester as a thriving centre, tammies and shalloons in Yorkshire, perpetuanas and serges in Devon. The Devonshire serge industry had indeed enjoyed a remarkable boom to become by 1700 one of the biggest branches of the English textile industry [32]. The old Norwich worsted industry had been revivified and branched out into the making of sundry mixed fabrics generally known as 'Norwich stuffs'. None of these changes, it must be stressed, was based on major technical innovation; none significantly changed the capital structure. They were not so much innovations as mutations. They may well have been helped along by changes in the nature of English wool [16], consequent upon agricultural changes. But the same basic features of the pre-industrialised society still held; and the new draperies – even more labour-intensive than the old draperies – offered work.

After the Flemish and Dutch immigrants of the sixteenth century the next to improve English textile production were the Huguenots from France, a trickle after the 1660s, a flow after the revocation of the Edict of Nantes in 1685. This time it was the turn of linen and silk to receive the advantages of skilled workers with knowledge of different variations upon old themes, and able to show the way towards the production of fabrics higher in quality than the poor wares which were the current staples of these English trades. The famous London settlement of French Huguenot silk workers in Spitalfields, which was to decline into a poverty-stricken slum in the nineteenth century, dates from this time; the English linen industry, which was to grow substantially in the course of the eighteenth century, was given a considerable boost in later Stuart times [30]. One part of that boost, for both linen and silk, was substantial protection against French imports : here were two prime examples of industries advancing by what economists call import-substitution.

But the foreign influences do not end here. One of the most remarkable stimuli to the English textile industries came from the astonishing fashionableness of the imported Indian cotton fabrics which were flooded into Europe by the English and Dutch East India Companies in the second half of the seventeenth century [26]. In later Stuart times the English East India Company's imports of all types of Asiatic textiles averaged over half a million pieces per year, and reached a high point of over a million pieces in the mid-1680s – an immense increase upon early seventeenth-century imports. Though many were re-exported, the impact on the native textile industry was formidable. The fashion for calicoes, muslins, chintzes, for bright prints and flowered cottons, was equalled only by the furious outcry from entrenched interests, aided by those who affected to see in it all a sign of decay in English morality and the rise of wicked luxury. The upshot was limited protection, by Acts of 1700 and 1721, and a significant stimulus to efforts to imitate these exotic products. The results were not very great in our period, but they provided

31

a useful base for the subsequent development of the textile-printing industry, mainly in London; and, still more important, they furthered the use of cotton in the Lancashire industry. As English participation in the slave trade developed, Lancashire manufacturers [23] tried to make English versions of the Indian cotton fabrics sold in Africa and worn by Africans, slave or free. Thus, by wider trading contacts, by the imitation of foreign fabrics, by the immigration of foreign artisans, was the English textile industry made more varied and a solid base for future development created.

One other branch of textiles demands attention: hosiery. Here we have a striking example of a technical innovation of the period which helped to foster the transformation of an essentially 'craft' industry into a putting-out pattern. The knitting of stockings from local wools, coarse and fine, producing hosiery greatly varying in quality and type, established itself during the sixteenth century in many counties of England, from the Lake District to the Cotswolds, from Yorkshire to Devon [31]. Much of the work was the by-employment of small-holding peasants. Their products were bought by merchants and a slowly emerging group of recognisable hosiers who dealt in products varying from high-class and fashionable silk stockings knitted in London to the coarse wares of the north. The invention in the 1590s by a Cambridge University-educated parson, William Lee, of the knitting frame is one of those bits of individual enterprise which happily defy efforts to fit them into explanatory schemes. Whatever its motivation, it caught on, for silk stockings in London and for worsted hosiery in Leicestershire and Nottinghamshire, Lee's home county. The frame could be used in the home, but it was a relatively expensive and complex device (it cost more than an ordinary hand-loom, for example) and so was often hired out by masters to domestic knitters [43]. Thus by the end of our period there was emerging, in hosiery as in other branches of the textile industry, a proletariat of industrial workers dependent upon a central capitalist for yarn, for knitting frames, for credit, and for markets.

Textiles provide the clearest exemplar of the putting-out system. It would be tedious to plod through all the other areas where it was to be found, or where craft activities were gradually penetrated by commercial enterprise and subjected to this new reign of the market. But one final and important instance must be mentioned : the making of small metal wares. In the 1540s it was said of Birmingham by a contemporary traveller that 'a great part of the Towne is maintained by Smiths, who have their iron and sea-cole out of Staffordshire' [44]. Little more than a village then, this future centre of the 'Black Country' of the nineteenth century was already in a region which, incorporating parts of the counties of Warwickshire, Worcestershire, Staffordshire and Shropshire, was gradually acquiring recognition as the metal-wares centre of the country. The resources of iron and coal combined with the vital transport nerve system of the Severn valley to provide its economic rationale. The ironmonger was the characteristic trader and entrepreneur; scythesmiths, blacksmiths, stirrup-makers, lorimers, and all manner of metal-workers, above all the ubiquitous nailer, abounded in an area notably free from gild control. But, again, the structure of an industry characterised by small masters and artisans was to be transformed into one of domestic capitalism, largely through the agency of a crucial invention : the slitting-mill. Introduced from the continent at the end of the sixteenth century, its use spread into the West Midlands by the 1620s. Its vital economic function was to link the output of the capital-intensive smelting and forging end of the iron industry with the input of the labour-intensive metal-manufacturing end of the industry. It did this by providing a water-powered method of slitting bar-iron into the narrow rods used by the makers of nails and other small metal goods, thereby replacing the laborious hand method of splitting iron which had hitherto been necessary. The introduction of such a device had a double effect : it raised productivity, and it facilitated the rapid domination of an industry by the capitalists who controlled the supply of the essential raw material. By the end of the seventeenth century 'prodigious numbers' of nailers were to be found in

Staffordshire and adjacent areas; men and boys worked up the iron rods in their own cottages, returning the finished products to the putters-out of rod-iron, who in turn supplied a growing trade, at home and overseas [44].

In this particular industry the exception which proves the rule of decentralisation is the remarkable enterprise of Ambrose Crowley [40]. This son of a midland nailer turned his back on his native area, went to the north-east, and in the 1690s set up near Newcastle a business which was to incorporate factories, warehouses, forges, a slitting-mill and a steel furnace, to turn out nails, tools, anchors and a range of miscellaneous wares. The rationale of this exceptional development lay not so much in labour or raw-material supply, however, as in access both to the best method of transport and to a special market. For Crowley (who blossomed into Sir Ambrose) effectively cornered the market in supplying the Navy with these requirements; and its dockyards were in the south and accessible by coastal trade. Thus scale and location of enterprise were dependent upon state demand – something also to be found in centralised production to which we must now turn.

4 *Centralised Production*

I

It is not possible to put a blast-furnace – even a seventeenth-century one – in a cottage, or to disperse the assembly process inherent in the building of a great house or a great ship. Such statements may seem so trite as to be pointless. The reason for making them is simply to stress the dependence of industrial organisation at any one time on prevailing techniques. When independent or quasi-independent artisans or some sort of putting-out arrangements were so common in manufacture, why did some industrial activities depart from the norm?

The essential features of centralised production and the necessary conditions of its functioning may be set out as they were for the putting-out system. Four basic technical conditions may be discerned, which would not merely facilitate some sort of centralisation, but would require it. First, it may be that the productive plant is a piece of fixed capital equipment to which the raw materials have to be brought for processing in some way. The furnace, be it for glass-making or lead-smelting or similar processes, is perhaps the most obvious example, though the category must also include sundry boiling or steeping processes, such as those involved in dyeing, soap-making, or the preparation of such substances as alum or starch. Second, the productive plant may be driven by power, normally in this period that of wind or falling water. Because such forms of power – like that of steam or atmospheric pressure, just arriving or soon to follow – were not transmissible over distances, as is electric power, so again it was necessary for all the inputs of the productive process to be taken to the plant, in brief for production to be centralised. This category includes all those activities which can usefully be called 'mill industries', for example, paper-making or flour-milling.

35

Third, the production may be centralised for the simple reason that the essential process is mining or extraction. There is no need to dwell on this : mining provides an obvious example of an activity drawing in workers to a central place of work. Fourth, and last, production may take the form of an assembly process. The building of ships, in which a variety of parts have not only to be fashioned but also put together to make one of the larger capital objects of the day, provides a classical example of this particular sort of centralised industrial activity.

These conditions are technical, not economic. *They tell us nothing whatever about the optimum economic size or scale of any plant.* This cannot be too strongly emphasised because a great deal of nonsense has been written about so-called 'large-scale' production, allegedly forming part of an 'industrial revolution' in Tudor and Stuart England, simply on the basis of noticing that at this time some industries were emerging which did indeed require concentration of workers. Then, as now, what determined the scale of operations of particular plants in particular industries was the nature of the costs, in relation to the demand for the product, faced by each individual operator. And, for the most part, demand was neither big enough nor constant enough to justify really large-scale production, nor were economies of scale normally such as to make big units economically viable. In short, although large units were to be found they were not typical, indeed they could not be typical in the economic circumstances of the time. The typical unit, even in this general category of centralised production, was small, with numbers of workers fluctuating markedly over the year, varying according to the state of demand, according to the seasons, at the mercy of water-power affected by drought or floods. Just as in the putting-out industries, output was increased by the employment of more spinners, weavers, nailers, or the like, so in these industries the equivalent method was normally and initially to increase the number of small plants. There were big mines, big shipyards, big mills, employing scores, even hundreds of workers. Such things, like Stumpe's cloth-making enterprise of the 1540s, or John Spilman's paper-mill at Dartford in the 1580s, or Crowley's iron-working factory of the 1690s, attracted the attention of contemporaries precisely because they were unusual. But the characteristic centralised enterprise, throughout the period, was something much more like the paper-mill in Hertfordshire of which it was said, later in the eighteenth century, that the *average* employment was five men and a boy, but 'sometimes more, sometimes less, sometimes girls, sometimes women, sometimes men'.

Centralised production, by its nature, often called for more fixed capital than did such an industry as textiles. Only for the larger units or enterprises, however, did this necessitate methods of finance radically different from the familiar pattern of credit provision. That was to be found in centralised industry, too, for working capital. Moreover, it was often by loans or credit from friends, relatives, trading associates and co-religionists, that businessmen were able to raise the larger amounts for fixed capital. When still larger sums were required recourse was had to the partnership or, less frequently, the joint-stock company [4] – as yet without limited liability and a much less impersonal affair than the modern business corporation. In coal, iron, paper, and a number of other industries with some fixed capital needs, partnerships rose in importance in the course of the seventeenth century. The joint-stock company first appeared in English industry with the chartering of the Mines Royal and the Mineral and Battery Works in 1568 [50, 51], both with state support and an eye upon armaments, but although a few other examples later appeared, they remained rarities in industry.

Once again, of course, it is important to understand that this category of industrial organisation, or this defining of conditions for its functioning, was not in practice a rigid set of demarcations. The edges were blurred. The use of simple furnaces, for example, could and did give rise to circumstances of production indistinguishable from those of the artisan craftsman, like the goldsmith working in his shop or the baker at his oven; the windmill grinding corn, tended by that familiar figure of fact and legend the miller, represents family enterprise a long way from what seems typified by the idea of centralised production.

Mills came in two main sorts – wind and water – and with a bewildering variety of purposes and names: for fulling, slitting, or pumping; corn-mills, paper-mills, snuff-mills, and gig-mills, and more besides. They imparted power to such industrial processes as grinding, crushing, pounding or cutting. All necessarily involved some fixed capital equipment, but only a very few gave rise to large enterprises or had more than half-a-dozen or so workers dependent upon them. Many a mill was owned by the landlord; sometimes, early in the period, it was still the manorial mill to which the tenants brought their corn for grinding; but as such practices declined the mill was often rented out for more overtly industrial purposes. Neither the fulling-mill nor the slitting-mill, however, in themselves gave rise to concentrations of workers, for they were merely stages in a bigger chain of production processes which determined the shape of the industry.

The paper industry [54] provides an example of mills which did provide the bases for productive units. Paper-mills often started life as converted corn- or fulling-mills. In 1485 there were no paper-mills in England; by 1714, when the manufacture had just become the subject of an excise duty (thus providing data for historians) there were some 200 in England and Wales alone. Here was a process – or rather series of processes – which demanded centralisation. The linen and cotton rags, from which paper was made before the nineteenth-century discovery of wood-pulp, had to be mixed with water and pounded to pulp; the paper was made by hand from the pulp by skilled workers; then it had to be sized, finished, dried and packed. As in iron-smelting the setting up and operation of such a productive unit needed access to credit or capital outside the scope of the small man. It was not a labour-intensive industry, as was textile manufacture, so its location was determined by a combination of available water, of supplies of rags, and of markets for the finished products. Not surprisingly, many paper-mills were set up along river valleys in counties around London such as Buckinghamshire, Hertfordshire and Kent.

Ships and houses were two very characteristic items of capital investment in pre-industrialised England. They both involved the use of that vital constructional material of the age, timber; they existed in such a variety of sizes that they offer examples of the biggest and the smallest pieces of fixed capital in the economy; and their construction or maintenance likewise could cover a range which at one end of the scale demanded no more than the work of one or two artisans, at the other could, and did, involve hundreds, even thousands, of workers gathered together in the biggest centralised establishments of the day.

The building industry hardly existed as a recognisable separate entity, if only because it was overwhelmingly the work of innumerable individual craftsmen. The shack or cabin which housed the squatter on the waste, the poorest of the cottagers' crude dwellings of stud and mud : such buildings barely required skills beyond those needed for mere survival. One stage upwards, and the village carpenter is joined by the thatcher, and, in the areas where stone was more readily available than timber, by the mason, to bring together some crucial craft skills functioning in a simple 'artisan-system'. But, at the other extreme, the building of the great houses of the age was an assembly process drawing together carpenters, joiners, carvers, masons, glaziers, plumbers, plasterers, bricklayers and brickmakers, as well as many labourers, in massive undertakings. Building the houses and palaces of Tudor and Stuart England – Hatfield or Hampton Court, Wollaton, Hardwick, Chatsworth, Knole, not to speak of Blenheim and scores of lesser examples – created pockets of centralised employment, albeit temporary, on a substantial scale. And, if the rebuilding of London after the Great Fire helped to throw up the builder as a recognisable entreprenuer, it must never be forgotten that the sheer growth of London, from a city of the third or fourth rank to the greatest city in Europe itself stimulated the building industry.

As with houses, so with ships [57]. Throughout the whole period most ships were small ships – coasting or cross-channel vessels of 20 to 50 tons or even less – made by a shipwright and his helpers with simple tools in circumstances which hardly merit the name of a shipyard. Even the ordinary merchant ships, averaging around 150 tons, which plied on the international trade routes of the day, did not necessarily demand large shipbuilding enterprises. From the later fifteenth century onwards ships were getting bigger – not just the oddities, like Henry VIII's *Henry Grâce à Dieu* or the East India Company's *Trade's Increase* of 1609, both ships of around 1000 tons, built in imitation of Spanish models (and in fact too big) – but ordinary ships for ordinary purposes, ships coming to average 300 to 400 tons, like the colliers in the east-coast coal trade or the East Indiamen of the eighteenth century. Though the English mercantile marine multiplied perhaps six-fold in tonnage between the reigns of Elizabeth and Anne, English shipbuilding techniques generally lagged behind the best European practices; by no means all the merchant fleet was English-built, and in the later seventeenth century many of the older east-coast shipyards, such as those of Ipswich and Woolbridge, declined. Newcastle, Whitby, Bristol and above all, London, however, saw new and bigger yards come into being, including such unusually substantial enterprises as that of Sir Henry Johnson at Blackwall. Yet few yards, even amongst these, regularly employed large numbers of workers. They were centralised undertakings – utterly unlike the putting-out arrangements of the textile industry – but very few were 'large scale'.

The biggest marine undertakings of the day were not in the private sector but in the public: the naval dockyards [55, 56] where the biggest ships of the line were built and repaired. This was largely a development of the last century of our period, as the specialised man-of-war emerged to take on the role formerly carried out by the Tudor merchant ship, tricked out with a few cannon and forced into royal service. After the middle of the seventeenth century the yards at Harwich, Woolwich, Deptford, Chatham and Portsmouth were expanded to meet the rapidly-growing needs of more and more expensive naval warfare, to build and maintain the 1000-ton 'third-rates' which had become the standard naval vessels of the day. By 1700 Portsmouth and Chatham were each regularly employing well over 1000 men, Woolwich and Deptford over 600 each. Shipwrights, caulkers,

40

carpenters, boat-makers, plumbers and labourers were all atten-
dant upon a complex of docks, mast-houses, rope-walks and the
like, so that, as was said of Woolwich in 1711, the town was
'chiefly compos'd of Workmen and others employed in Her
Majesty's Dockyard, Ropeyard and Ordnance Service' [55].

IV

If the special and fluctuating demands of war helped to maintain
one sort of centralised industrial establishment, they also left
their mark on another branch of industry which, for quite other
reasons, also knew fixed capital investment of a type unusual in
pre-industrialised England.

The smelting of iron by means of the water-powered charcoal-
fuelled blast-furnace has figured in books about Tudor and Stuart
economic history as a classic example of early 'large-scale', cap-
italised industry. A concomitant and much-repeated argument
has it that throughout the period the country was also under-
going a 'timber-shortage' or 'fuel famine'; this was largely, if not
wholly, consequent upon the gobbling up of woodlands by the
demands of the blast-furnaces and similar wood eaters; the result,
so the story goes, was the rapid growth of coal-mining in England and of the use of coal as an alternative fuel, culminating in
the discovery, by Abraham Darby in about 1709, of how to smelt
iron with coked coal, thus revivifying an industry declining under
the weight of its fuel problem. Here is a neat sequence of economic problems and solutions, as well as a thread gratifyingly
connecting pre-industrialised England with the Industrial Revolution. It is a mixture of sense and nonsense.

Certainly it is true that the introduction of the blast-furnace
into England sometime towards the end of the fifteenth century [39], had the economic effect of putting a process of some
capital-intensity in a position from which it could dominate the
entire iron industry. The blast-furnace, together with its bellows
and the necessary water-wheel and water-courses, evolved into a
costly piece of fixed capital, especially when physically linked
with its adjunct, the finery forge, with water-powered tilt hammer.
The construction, maintenance, and operation of such a producing

unit was quite outside the financial range of those without access to capital and credit. So it is not surprising to find landlords on whose lands there happened to be the requisite inputs of iron-ore, water-power and charcoal, concerning themselves with the setting up of such iron works. Amongst them were the Sidneys in the Weald of Sussex, in the mid-sixteenth century; the Earl of Shrewsbury in Shropshire in the 1560s; the Earl of Rutland at Rievaulx in the 1570s; the Hanburys in South Wales in the 1580s and 1590s; the Brownes and Courthopes in seventeenth-century Kent and Sussex; and the great iron family of the late seventeenth century, the Foleys [41], who, through a series of inter-locking partnerships of friends and relatives, dominated the West Midlands industry, with their ownership of furnaces, forges, ware-houses, slitting-mills, and wire-works. But again we must be care-ful in assuming that because some such units were big, all were big. Some blast-furnaces, particularly early ones, were tiny and primitive affairs, with small output and low productivity. Many forges were small and separately owned, supplied with pig iron from other furnaces. Neither produced regular employment all the year round, for in the summer months there was often so little head of water that operations were impossible. Over the two cen-turies or so of our period, however, there was a substantial im-provement which went in the direction of larger furnaces and higher productivity, that is using less charcoal to produce more iron. Here we have an increase in the scale of operations, distinct from the fact of centralisation. Dr Hammersley's research on this subject [39] suggests that between the 1530s and 1540s and *circa* 1700 in the whole process of smelting and conversion of pig into bar-iron there was approximately a threefold improvement in the amount of iron produced with a given amount of charcoal. In the first three-quarters of the sixteenth century many small fur-naces were erected, mostly in the Weald of Sussex and Kent, so that of 67 identified furnaces in the 1570s, 52 were in that area. All told they perhaps produced around 13,000 tons. By the 1720s a total of 60 furnaces were probably producing approx-imately 25,000 tons; but only 13 were left in the Weald, the centre of the industry having moved to South Wales, the Forest of Dean, the West Midlands and Yorkshire [39].

This was not the achievement of a declining industry suffering from the exhaustion of English timber supplies. Between the later fifteenth and the mid-seventeenth century, while the prices of agricultural products in general rose over six-fold, timber prices rose only just over five-fold. Nevertheless, it was a high-cost industry, relative to the bigger iron-producing countries of Europe – Sweden, Russia and France – and it was supplying a decreasing proportion of a rapidly growing home demand. During the same period, when English output of iron had roughly doubled, import of bar-iron had risen about fifteen-fold, so that by the early eighteenth century England was regularly importing nearly 20,000 tons of bar-iron, mostly from Sweden. English furnaces met the substantial home demand for armaments – cannon, shot and the like – but more and more of the growing non-armament demand had to draw upon foreign supplies, especially for the higher quality iron needed in the making of the very small quantity of steel produced at that time. The reason for this disadvantageous position of the English industry was mainly the combination of the lower grade of ores used together with the continuing rise in fuel costs despite increased productivity. Fuel accounted for about 60 to 75 per cent of the total costs in the whole process of smelting and conversion to bar-iron. Between the 1590s and the 1690s charcoal prices probably rose about threefold, but in that rise what mattered most was not the price of wood but of transport and wages. We can be reasonably sure that far more woodland was cleared for growing food, pasturing animals or building houses or ships than was destroyed in the interests of the iron industry. Indeed, during the seventeenth century, improvements in forest management led to the conservation of coppices, from which the cordwood was derived for charcoal burning, as well as encouraging re-planting. But charcoal was fragile and bulky to transport; and the population upsurge, so useful to the labour-intensive textile industry which fitted so well into the family economy, was of little or no help to an industry dependent on the labour of charcoal burners and the technical prowess of furnace and forge operators. So costs of fuel varied from area to area, rising sharply with distance from the furnaces and forges. It was not a national fuel shortage, but a series of regional difficulties, consequent upon problems of accessibility. Yet the potentially alternative fuel, coal, was also bulky, heavy and costly to transport, though cheap at the pit-head. It seems reasonable to infer that coal could only become practicably attractive as an alternative fuel when and where there happened to be a close proximity of iron-ore, coal, and existing charcoal-fuelled iron-works. The possibility of this opened up when the industry began to concentrate in parts of the West Midlands though that was certainly not in itself enough to dislodge charcoal as a fuel. But a new situation was being created. It was well expressed by Andrew Yarranton's observations, made in 1677:

> Iron-works are so far from the destroying of woods and timber that they are the occasion of the increase thereof. For in all parts where iron works are, there generally are great quantities of pit coals very cheap, and in these places are great quantities of coppices or woods which supply the iron works; and if the iron works were not in being these coppices would have been stocked up and turned into pasture and tillage, as is now daily done in Sussex and Surrey, where the ironworks or most of them, are laid down.[2]

His remarks should serve to put into perspective the more publicised but exaggerated complaints about the iron industry destroying the Wealden woodlands in the later sixteenth and early seventeenth centuries.

Since about 1620 a number of experimenters, of whom the best known was Dud Dudley, who publicised his efforts in 1665, had tried to use coal for smelting iron. Whatever their failures or success, the industry had shown no particular interest. The same was for long true of Abraham Darby's invention [42]. That invention was important, but its immediate significance in our period was limited. Darby obtained a patent in 1707 for a particular way of casting pots. It had nothing to do with the use of coked coal as a fuel. All that is known, for certain, is that after taking over a furnace and forge at Coalbrookdale in Shropshire in 1709–10 he experimented successfully with the production of cast pots and similar utensils by means of iron smelted with coked

44

coal mined locally, though unsuccessfully with attempts to produce pig for the bar-iron trade. He and his successors built up a profitable casting business, using mineral fuel, but charcoal continued to be the main fuel of the iron industry, long after his death in 1717. But the very interest in coal as a smelting agent could never have come about without the substantial increase in the mining and use of coal in England which had been proceeding quite independently during the same period.

v

There was nothing new about mining in England, but in the sixteenth and seventeenth centuries its diverse output was, in some areas, so increased as to pose problems in a far more acute fashion than had ever happened earlier. Lead, tin and copper were, probably in that order, the most valuable of the non-ferrous metals mined in this country. Coal, rising rapidly in importance, has come to overshadow the others in historical retrospect. Lead came to surpass tin in its contribution to the country's export trade. Mined in various areas, particularly Yorkshire, Derbyshire, Wales and parts of the south-west, the metallic lead obtained from smelting the ore found its way into diverse uses including building and type-founding, glass-making, pottery and paint or as an alloy in the pewter from which so many domestic utensils were made [46]. Its markets were thus in London and in the growing industrial areas such as the West Midlands and Newcastle; but the ore was found in mainly remote or mountainous regions. So here was a typical problem of the mining industry – the costs of transport, be they of ore, of fuel for smelting, or of final product. The ancient tin-mining industry of Cornwall [47, 48] had to import charcoal but its proximity to the sea aided the shipment of both the fuel and the tin to London. Similar problems arose in copper, mined in Cornwall, Wales and the Lake District; in shifting the ore to the smelters, heavily concentrated in South Wales; and in the location of the industry of making brass (an alloy of copper and zinc), much in demand for cannon [49].

To contemporary travellers and foreign visitors the mining of coal seemed one of the most striking of English economic phenomena. Despite its antiquity, only by the later sixteenth century was it beginning to have some real significance for the economy as a whole. In pursuit of the laudable intent of demonstrating that significance with facts and figures, some very exaggerated statements have been made about this growth of coal-mining in our period, and a spurious 'industrial revolution' erected upon these flimsy foundations. They demand some investigation, partly because they provide classic illustrations of how not to use numbers in history, and partly because their dubiousness may even detract from the very significance of what they are supposed to illuminate.

All the main coalfields except Kent were in use, but the Northumberland and Durham field was almost certainly of overwhelming importance. By the end of the seventeenth century it may have been producing something approaching a half of the country's whole output. Its proximity to the sea facilitated easy coastwise trade, and for our knowledge of the size of its output we are dependent on the records of coastal trade. The same is true, on a much smaller scale and much more inaccurately, for other fields whose output can be identified in the trade of particular ports. Only in the very few cases where colliery records survive is it possible to check or augment these records. This means that we have little or no quantitative information about the output of the inland coalfields of the Midlands. Yet it has been asserted that there was a fourteen-fold increase in total English coal output between mid-Tudor and later Stuart times; and, for the Northumberland and Durham field, that 'in less than a century and a quarter, shipments from Newcastle multiplied nearly nineteenfold, while imports at London multiplied more than thirtyfold' [34]. The former statement is a guess: no more, no less. The latter statement, although derived from contemporary figures for the coasting trade, gets the high rates of growth by the simple magic of comparing single years: namely 1563–4 and 1684–5, for Newcastle shipments; and 1580 (or to be more precise an adjustment of six and a half months of that year) and 1697–8, for London imports. To have even the sketchy significance which dubious contemporary statistics can impart, comparisons over such long periods must be based on some sort of

46

averages. Using, when possible, four- or five-year averages of Professor Nef's own published figures [34, II, Appendix D], a comparison of the 1590s with the 1690s yields an increase in Newcastle's coastal exports of coal *not* of nineteen-fold but of rather over three-fold; and for London's imports between the 1580s and the first decade of the eighteenth century *not* of thirty-fold but of roughly fifteen-fold. A recent article by Dr Langton [36] based on detailed records of the South-West Lancashire coalfield reveals a similar order of exaggeration. Of this field, Nef asserted that the output had increased about fifteen-fold between 1550 and 1700. Dr Langton shows that a much more likely rate of change from the 1590s to the 1680s lay between two- and four-fold, and the really rapid increase in output came much later in the eighteenth century.

What these calculations suggest is, first, that relatively high rates of growth may well have been achieved for English coal output and trade between, say, the 1480s and 1580s when absolute quantities were still very small; but we have no reliable figures to support this reasonable guess. Second, it is likely that while London's seaborne imports of coal from the Northumberland and Durham field were indeed growing rapidly, total English output of coal during the period as a whole was rising at a much more moderate pace. That this should be so is supported by the disproportionate growth in London's population – perhaps ten- or twelve-fold while that of the country as a whole rose only two- or three-fold – as well as by the widespread contemporary usage of the term 'sea-cole'. The spectacular growth of the east-coast coal trade attracted much attention; and so did the rise of Newcastle itself, hailed by Celia Fiennes in 1697 as 'a noble town' that 'most resembles London of any place in England'.[3] *Circa* 1700 the total annual output of coal was perhaps about $2\frac{1}{2}$m. tons. This is rather less than half a ton per head; in 1900 it was around 6 tons per head for a greatly enlarged population. By that time it had become the vital fuel for an industrialised economy. In our period it was still overwhelmingly a cheap fuel for the poor, to warm their hearths in any areas where wood was scarce and dear and where water-transport could make coal cheap. Witness to the importance of this demand comes from the complaints by Londoners, certainly as early as 1590, against the rising prices of 'sea-cole' and the monopoly thereof exercised by the body known as the Hostmen of Newcastle.

Nevertheless, the use of coal for industrial purposes certainly increased during Tudor and Stuart times [34]; and in those limited circumstances in which it could be used, this may well have facilitated lowered costs and growth in output, to the advantage of England relative to certain continental industries. As an industrial fuel its use implied some sort of fixed capital equipment; consequently the industries in which it came to replace charcoal fall into our centralised category. The use of coal in salt-making by the evaporation of brine (notably on the north-east coast) was well under way in the later sixteenth century; the manufacture of alum, copperas, and saltpetre all came to employ it during the seventeenth century; it replaced charcoal on all sorts of processes in which the simple matter of raising the temperature of a liquid was of central importance, for example soap-boiling, starch-making, sugar-refining or dyeing; after the mid-seventeenth century coked coal was more and more used in malting. The brewing of beer – gradually becoming, from the sixteenth century onwards, a form of centralised production as it used hops as a preservative and was thus distinguished from the truly domestic brewing of ale – began to use coal as it grew up in London and in provincial towns accessible to river- or sea-borne transport of coal [53]. A number of technical problems in the use of coal were solved: the English glass-making industry pioneered the coal-fired furnace in the early seventeenth century [52]; coal became more common in brick-making in the later part of the century; a coal-fired furnace for lead smelting was patented in 1693; and in the early eighteenth century similar successes were attained not only with iron but with the smelting of tin.

In all these developments the cost of transport was of vital consequence, for coal, like other minerals and other high-bulk/low-value inputs (stone, timber, charcoal), depended on water transport to make its use worthwhile at any distance far from the place of origin. So one of the consequences of the growing consumption of coal, as well as of other products of the extractive industries, was to add greatly to existing stimuli to water-borne trade, to the coastal trade, and to improving the navigability of rivers.

Mining had other important consequences. The deeper the mine, the greater were the problems of haulage (of miners and ore alike), of ventilation, and of drainage. Risk increased and so did the cost of the enterprise; greater capital was needed; and more ingenuity was put to resolving the difficulties by technical innovation. Again, we must be careful to distinguish between the typical and the exceptional, to separate the mere fact of centralisation from the scale of operations. Some of the biggest coal-mining enterprises, in Northumberland, Durham and Cumberland, brought fortunes to such landowners as the Lowthers or the Liddells, employed hundreds of workers and embodied substantial capital outlays in pits which in a few cases, had reached a depth of 400 feet. Conversely many a West Midland or South Wales undertaking had a few tiny pits worked by less than a dozen men in each. It was the problem of mine drainage which stimulated, right at the end of Stuart times, the momentous innovation of the atmospheric engine, precursor of the steam engine. For all the theoretical and experimental work done in London, in Paris, and elsewhere, the two men who made the effective breakthrough – Thomas Savery and, especially, Thomas Newcomen – were setting out to solve the specific practical difficulties of mine and colliery owners. Savery's engine, advertised as 'The Miner's Friend' in 1702 proved unsuccessful in practice; Newcomen, a Devonian aware of the acute drainage problems of deep Cornish tin mines, had more luck or skill. By 1716 atmospheric engines of his design were pumping water from a few of the country's coal and tin mines.

5 Conclusion

Until about 1650 industrial expansion was sustained, though not created, by the population increase and by the inflation which, though mild by modern standards, had pushed up food prices about six-fold since the 1480s. The combination of the two in the economic circumstances of the England of the time had the general effect of enlarging the labour force and lowering the real wages of those unable to take advantage of the rising prices. Those who could – and they were to be found in a wide range of society from minor yeomen to important noblemen – increased their incomes, certainly in money terms and often in real terms, thus enabling them to purchase more of the products of industry. Meanwhile, those with holdings of land too small to take advantage of rising food prices, or with no land at all, turned increasingly to industry to try to close the gap in their real earnings. Industry, already vigorous though limited in extent and variety, was thus favoured with an increased labour supply and with markets expanding at home and abroad. This incentive to industrial growth brought no concomitant incentive to increase productivity by the substitution of capital for labour.

After the middle of the seventeenth century the economic context altered. The true course of population change remains unknown, but there seems good reason to suppose that overall growth slackened perhaps to the point of a stagnant population, though a number of trading towns continued to grow in size and wealth. Similarly the price rise stopped, even went into reverse for some goods for some periods. Despite harvest failures periodically bringing high prices, the generally downward movement of the cost of food was such that real wages rose slightly. For employers and manufacturers a squeeze between the prices of factors and of final products was beginning to make its presence felt. Complaints of shortages of industrial labour ('want of hands') were heard, sometimes perhaps more of a symptom than a reality, as well as grumbles about the allegedly idle habits of working men and women. Complex changes in overseas trade were bringing shifts in the demand for industrial products; new groupings of wealth and population were affecting it internally; the unprecedentedly expensive wars which accompanied the end of the Stuart reigns brought, directly or indirectly, stimuli to some sectors and difficulties to others; the search for revenue to finance the wars raised import tariffs thus also providing protection to several industries. The country's manufacturing activity was growing more diverse in an economic conjuncture which increasingly called for some substitution of capital for labour, for greater ingenuity in methods of raising productivity or in adapting the product to changing markets. The following quotation from a contemporary merchant writing in 1695 will serve to summarise what was in the air :

> . . . the glass maker hath found a quicker way of making it out of things which cost him little or nothing. Silk stockings are wove instead of knit. Tobacco is cut by engines instead of knives. Books are printed instead of written. Deal boards are sawn with a mill instead of men's labour. . . .
>
> New projections are every day set on foot to render the making our manufactures easy, which are made cheap by the heads of the manufacturers, not by falling the price of poor people's labour. . . .[4]

It was not all so easy or so evident as John Cary's words suggest. It brought no industrial revolution in his time. But it pointed to the way of the future.

References

1. Quoted in T. S. Willan, *The Early History of the Russia Company, 1553–1603*, (Manchester, 1956) pp. 246–7.
2. Andrew Yarranton, *England's Improvement by Sea and Land* (London, 1677).
3. C. Morris (ed.), *The Journeys of Celia Fiennes* (London, 1947) p. 209.
4. John Cary, *An Essay on the State of England* (London, 1695); quoted in *Seventeenth Century Economic Documents*, ed. J. Thirsk and J. P. Cooper (Oxford, 1972) pp. 322–3.

Select Bibliography

This is not an exhaustive book-list nor does it include any of the general works on the economic history of the period which contain chapters on industry. For an alternative general account, with a longer and very good bibliography, see L. A. Clarkson, *The Pre-Industrial Economy in England, 1500–1750*, especially Chapter 4 and its relevant bibliographical section.

I GENERAL

[1] J. Thirsk, 'Industries in the Countryside' in *Essays in the Economic and Social History of Tudor and Stuart England*, ed. F. J. Fisher (Cambridge, 1961).
An important article, seeking to explain the location of rural industry.

[2] E. L. Jones, 'Agricultural Origins of Industry', *Past and Present*, 40 (1968).

[3] G. Unwin, *Industrial Organization in the Sixteenth and Seventeenth Centuries* (London, 1904; reprinted 1957).
An old book but still full of insight and interest.

[4] W. R. Scott, *The Constitution and Finance of English, Scottish and Irish Joint-Stock Companies to 1720*, 3 vols (Cambridge, 1910–12).
A work for reference, but full of valuable information about joint-stock ventures in industry between 1553 and 1720.

[5] C. Singer *et al.* (eds), *A History of Technology, 1500–1750*, vol. III (Oxford, 1953).
Another work of reference, not always accurate or even plausible on economic interpretation, but useful on all sorts of technical matters.

[6] D. C. Coleman, 'Technology and Economic History, 1500–1750', *Economic History Review*, 2nd ser., XI (1959).
A review article on [5].

[7] J. U. Nef, 'The Progress of Technology and the Growth of

large-scale Industry in Great Britain, 1540–1640', *Economic History Review*, v (1934).*
The *locus classicus* of the idea of 'large-scale' industry in this period. Derived from [34].

[8] D. C. Coleman, 'Industrial Growth and Industrial Revolutions', *Economica* (February 1956).*
An attack on [7] and on the proliferation of 'industrial revolutions' generally.

II CRAFTS AND GILDS

[9] S. Kramer, *The English Craft Gilds* (New York, 1927).
A very useful survey although the generalisations are too general.

[10] G. Unwin, *The Gilds and Companies of London* (London, 1908).

[11] J. R. Kellett, 'The Breakdown of Gild and Corporation Control over the Handicraft and Retail Trade in London', *Economic History Review*, 2nd ser., x (1958).

[12] D. M. Palliser, 'The Trade Gilds of Tudor York', in *Crisis and Order in English Towns, 1500–1700*, ed. P. Clark and P. Slack (London, 1972).

[13] C. Phythian-Adams, 'Ceremony and the Citizen: the Communal Year at Coventry, 1450–1550', in *Crisis and Order*, ed. Clark and Slack.
Two interesting recent articles on the survival of gilds in the sixteenth century and on their ritual aspects. The collection in which they appear has some other chapters which touch on industrial matters.

[14] L. A. Clarkson 'The Organisation of the English Leather Industry in the late Sixteenth and Seventeenth centuries', *Economic History Review*, 2nd ser., XIII (1960).

[15] —— 'The Leather Crafts in Tudor and Stuart England', *Agricultural History Review*, XIV (1960).
A pair of articles on a neglected but important craft.

III TEXTILES

General

[16] P. J. Bowden, *The Wool Trade in Tudor and Stuart England* (London, 1962).

* Reprinted in E. M. Carus-Wilson (ed.), *Essays in Economic History* (London, 1954, 1962) vols 1 and 3 respectively.

[17]   D. W. Jones, 'The "Hallage" Receipts of the London Cloth Markets, 1562–c.1720', *Economic History Review*, 2nd ser., xxv (1972).
A valiant and valuable attempt to use the statistics of the Blackwell Hall cloth sales.

[18]   C. Wilson, 'Cloth Production and International Competition in the seventeenth century', *Economic History Review*, 2nd ser., xiii (1960).

[19]   D. C. Coleman, 'An Innovation and its Diffusion: the "New Draperies" ', *Economic History Review*, 2nd ser., xxii (1969).

[20]   N. B. Harte and K. Ponting (eds), *Textile History and Economic History* (Manchester, 1973).
See especially the two chapters mentioned below: [30] and [31].

Regional and Particular

[21]   H. Heaton, *The Yorkshire Woollen and Worsted Industries* (Oxford, 1920).

[22]   N. Lowe, *The Lancashire Textile Industry in the Sixteenth Century* (Manchester, 1972).

[23]   J. de L. Mann, *The Cloth Industry in the West of England from 1640 to 1880* (Oxford, 1971).

[24]   G. D. Ramsay, *The Wiltshire Woollen Industry in the Sixteenth and Seventeenth Centuries* (Oxford, 1943, reprinted London, 1965).

[25]   A. P. Wadsworth and J. de L. Mann, *The Cotton Trade and Industrial Lancashire, 1600–1780* (Manchester, 1931; reprinted London, 1965).

[26]   A. W. Douglas, 'Cotton textiles in England: the East India Company's Attempt to Exploit Developments in Fashion, 1660–1721', *Journal of British Studies*, viii (1969).

[27]   T. C. Mendenhall, *The Shrewsbury Drapers and the Welsh Wool Trade in the Sixteenth and Seventeenth Centuries* (Oxford, 1953).

[28]   G. Unwin, *Studies in Economic History*, Part ii, chap. 7 ('The History of the Cloth Industry in Suffolk') (London, 1927).

[29]   J. E. Pilgrim, 'The Rise of the "New Draperies" in Essex', *University of Birmingham Historical Journal*, vii (1959–60).

[30]   N. B. Harte, 'The Rise of Protection and the English Linen Trade, 1690–1790', in [20].

[31]   J. Thirsk, 'The Fantastical Folly of Fashion: the English Stocking Knitting Industry, 1500–1700', in [20].

[32]   W. B. Stephens, *Seventeenth Century Exeter* (Exeter, 1958).
[33]   W. H. Chaloner, 'Sir Thomas Lombe and the British Silk Industry', in his *People and Industries* (London, 1963).

IV   COAL AND IRON

[34]   J. U. Nef, *The Rise of the British Coal Industry*, (London, 1932; reprinted 1966) (2 vols).
       The definitive (?) work on the subject, but full of exaggerations. Use with care. Develops the idea of an 'industrial revolution' in this period.
[35]   T. S. Ashton and J. Sykes, *The Coal Industry of the Eighteenth Century* (Manchester, 1929; reprinted 1964).
[36]   J. L. Langton, 'Coal Output in South-West Lancashire, 1590–1799', *Economic History Review*, 2nd ser., xxv (1972).
[37]   H. R. Schubert, *History of the British Iron and Steel Industry* (London, 1957).
[38]   M. W. Flinn, 'The Growth of the English Iron Industry 1660–1760', *Economic History Review*, 2nd ser., xi (1958).
[39]   G. Hammersley, 'The Charcoal Iron Industry and its Fuel, 1540–1750', *Economic History Review*, 2nd ser., xxvi (1973).
       These two articles provide a major revision of accepted views on the English iron industry, that by Hammersley, based on lengthy research, being particularly important.
[40]   M. W. Flinn, *Men of Iron: The Crowleys in the Early Iron Industry* (Edinburgh, 1962).
[41]   B. L. C. Johnson, 'The Foley Partnerships: the Iron Industry at the End of the Charcoal Era', *Economic History Review*, 2nd ser., iv (1952).
[42]   A. Raistrick, *Dynasty of Iron Founders: the Darbys and Coalbrookdale* (London, 1953; reprinted Newton Abbot, 1970).

V   OTHERS AND VARIOUS

[43]   J. D. Chambers, *The Vale of Trent, 1670–1800*, Supplement No. 3 to the *Economic History Review* (Cambridge, 1957).
[44]   W. H. B. Court, *The Rise of the Midland Industries* (Oxford, 1938).
[45]   C. W. Chalkin, *Seventeenth Century Kent* (London, 1965).
       These three regional studies deal with several sorts of industries.

[46] R. Burt, 'Lead Production in England and Wales, 1700–70', *Economic History Review*, 2nd ser., xxii (1969).

[47] J. Hatcher, *English Tin Production and Trade before 1550* (Oxford, 1973).

[48] G. R. Lewis, *The Stannaries* (Boston, 1908; reprinted Truro, 1965).

[49] H. Hamilton, *The English Brass and Copper Industries to 1880* (London, 1926; reprinted 1967).

[50] M. B. Donald, *Elizabethan Copper. The History of the Company of Mines Royal, 1568–1605* (Oxford, 1955).

[51] —— *Elizabethan Monopolies. The History of the Company of Mineral and Battery Works, 1568–1604* (Edinburgh and London, 1961).

[52] D. W. Crossley, 'The Performance of the Glass Industry in the sixteenth century', *Economic History Review*, 2nd ser., xxv (1972).

[53] P. Mathias, *The Brewing Industry in England, 1700–1830* (Cambridge, 1959).

[54] D. C. Coleman, *The British Paper Industry, 1495–1860* (Oxford, 1958).

[55] —— 'Naval Dockyards under the Later Stuarts', *Economic History Review*, 2nd ser., vi (1953).

[56] J. Ehrman, *The Navy in the War of William III* (Cambridge, 1953).
Book and article together show something of the considerable economic impact of the Navy and the nature of its establishments.

[57] R. Davis, *The Rise of the English Shipping Industry in the Seventeenth and Eighteenth Centuries* (London, 1962; reprinted Newton Abbot, 1972).

Index